WILD MUSHROOM ON A BUDGET

Our Best Saving Money Tips

CHARLES J. BROWN

CONTENTS

INTRODUCTION

Large restaurants and hotels frequently serve wonderful meals made of mushrooms. They consume corpses to produce their nutrient-rich meal. Not all varieties of wild mushrooms can be consumed. Edible wild mushrooms can be grown at home and are particularly safe for human consumption. The woodland is home to a veritable jungle of mushroom species, including the penny bun, puffballs, shaggy inkcaps, and many more.

You should use caution when looking for them in your spare time. Additionally poisonous, these plants should not be touched if you have never seen them before. Would you be interested in raising these plants? Becoming a farmer requires a long trip since you must first seek education.

Before cultivating edible wild mushrooms for sale, you

need to gather a lot of information. The species are very diverse; some resemble one another as briefly noted. This means that it's simple to mistake something harmful for something edible. It is essential to learn enough about each species to determine whether it is suitable for human consumption.

The same is true for mothers who adore cooking mushroom-based meals for their families frequently. First and foremost, one must develop the habit of never touching or eating any plant that resembles a mushroom. When picking it, perhaps one should wear gloves. Next, present it to the professionals so they can assist in determining its biological categorization.

You should be aware of a lot of advice when dealing with this natural vegetation. Get some decent gloves first if you want to start gathering these plants for food so that your skin won't encounter any dangerous mushrooms. You will encounter many different species in the forest; therefore, it is best to avoid mixing them in one container. As a result, the non-deadly species wouldn't become contaminated by the poisonous ones.

Find some paper to wrap the foods to preserve their nutritional value; however, plastic bags should be avoided since they will impede appropriate airflow. Although harvesting is undoubtedly a fun hobby, you should avoid destroying the ecosystem. Simply uproot the entire plant, as trimming it would encourage the dispersion of spores.

If you make a mess, put it in a basket and throw it

away from where the edibles are coming from. You need to be quite cautious when cooking. Purchase unusual kitchenware, like the mushroom cleaning brush. Clean any beautifully shaped items with the brush after removing any insects or trash.

After cleaning, you can store the edible wild mushrooms in the refrigerator for subsequent preparation. These plants will fully dry after being frozen, allowing you to store them in tins with tight lids. The method of preparation would probably depend on the recipes one chooses to test. There are several recipes available that originate from well-known chefs. When looking for information and recipes for each species, use the internet.

CHAPTER ONE

*Recipes for mushrooms -
Storage*

The usage of various types of mushrooms as a component in a wide range of culinary endeavors has dramatically increased in recent decades.

Of course, those of us who enjoy mushrooms will be happy about this. For a while, fans were continuously upset to see mushrooms that had been improperly prepared or that were frequently used as a plate-filling garnish and looked unpleasant.

All that has changed lately because of the enormous increase in mushroom recipes and information, as well as the growing public and professional recognition of the health benefits of many kinds of fungus.

However, there is still room for improvement in how they are used in the normal household, namely in storage.

If you want to get fresh mushrooms at their best, their shelf life in a home isn't very long. To make sure they are in good condition when using them in your mushroom recipes, there are a few simple guidelines you can adhere to.

In passing, be aware that there isn't always consensus on this issue.

Some people have peculiar ideas on how to store fresh mushrooms, so you might have to follow your judgment based on several slightly different pieces of advice.

• You may keep them in the refrigerator for up to three days, usually. To prevent them from drying out, try to do it somewhere other than a plastic bag, but make sure they are softly covered with some kitchen towel.

• They can also be kept for several days at room temperature. Again, resist the need to place them in that freezer bag; instead, place them in a regular paper bag so they can breathe. You can leave them open on the shelf, as you might see in a grocery store if there is some air circulation, but it's still a good idea to keep them gently covered to prevent drying tendencies.

• When gathering wild mushrooms, put them in an open basket made of straw or some other material rather than a plastic bag. This helps them keep their freshness while also allowing their spores to move through the air as you move. Of course, unless you are knowledgeable on how to recognize potentially deadly mushrooms or have someone with you who is, you should never collect and eat wild mushrooms.

• Although dried mushrooms can usually be stored for a lot longer if maintained in an airtight container, it goes without saying that this is not always the case. Keep in mind that some recipes call for soaking dried varieties of mushrooms before using them.

• When a plant is past its prime, watch for brown damp patches on the cap, stalks that appear limp and lifeless, or a shriveled appearance on the cap or stalks. Additionally, keep an eye out for any sizable regions of gill discoloration.

Nothing in the foregoing is intended to imply that this is a difficult technical problem. In contrast, storage is simple if you use common sense, and your mushroom recipes will benefit from receiving ingredients that are in excellent shape!

CHAPTER TWO

Recipe for Wild Risotto

If served with salad, this vibrant risotto is a great, healthful main course for a dinner party. A vegan version is as simple to make.

Vegetable stock, 1 liter/134 quarts (you may need more)
Olive oil, 10ml/2 tsp.
375g/12 oz of finely chopped onion with arborio rice
Dry white wine in 150ml (5 fl oz)
15g/1/2 ounces of dried cep mushrooms/1/2 ounces of butter (or vegan margarine, if making the vegan recipe)
225g/8oz mixed wild mushrooms, 50g/2oz cooked Camargue red wild rice, sliced 100g/4oz wild rice, and

50g/2oz cooked vegetarian pecorino cheese (optional –

omit for vegan recipes)
To taste, add salt and freshly ground black pepper.
1. In a big pot, bring the stock to a boil and then simmer it.

2. Fry the onion in a separate, large pot with hot oil until it is tender and just beginning to color. While constantly stirring, add the arborio rice and simmer for 2 minutes.

3. Add the wine, then simmer for 5 minutes. Using a big ladle, start adding the stock. Before adding the next ladle full of stock, cook gently while stirring frequently and making sure that all the stock has been absorbed. It ought to take 25 to 30 minutes.
4. Cover the ceps with boiling water and let them soak for 15 to 20 minutes while the rice is cooking. Chop after draining while saving the soaking liquid. Sliced wild

mushrooms are swiftly cooked in a frying pan with heated butter or vegan margarine for around 5 minutes. Add the two cooked wild rice, all of the mushrooms, and the soaking liquid to the rice. If more stock is required, add some and fully cook the dish.

5. After turning off the heat, add the pecorino cheese if

using. Serve right away after seasoning to taste.

Best practice: The soaking liquid for dried mushrooms is

flavorful. Before adding it to a dish, it is a good idea to strain it through fine muslin because the mushrooms may have left behind a gritty residue.

13

CHAPTER THREE

Chicken Breasts in a Sage and Wild Mushroom Sauce

Chicken and wild mushrooms are a match made in paradise, and sage enhances both flavors nicely. If you don't have fresh sage, though, you may substitute French or Russian tarragon or basil. No formula is set in stone,

and I occasionally use mixed mushrooms or a variety of wild mushrooms depending on my mood. Although I have used it with guinea fowl, I haven't tried it with turkey breast, but I assume it would be fantastic. Before roasting, I occasionally add wrap parma or serrano ham around the chicken breasts.

Ingredients

3 teaspoons of butter
three shallots, diced

ten ounces of cremini mushrooms and one teaspoon of
fresh parsley, diced
1 glass of dry vermouth
Double cream, 1 cup
a sizable handful of finely minced, purple-leafed sage
one teaspoon of olive oil
Chicken breasts weighing half a pound, Kosher salt, and
freshly ground black pepper

Set the oven to 375 degrees Fahrenheit.
On a metal baking sheet, place the chicken breasts,
sprinkle with olive oil, season well, and roast for 20
minutes, or until done. Butter should be melted while the
shallots are sautéing for a minute. Five additional minutes
of sautéing are required to brown the mushrooms after
adding the parsley and mushrooms. Deglazing the pan
with vermouth while scraping up any fragments that may
be stuck to the bottom of the pan. Add the cream and stir.
The sauce should be brought to a simmer and reduced
until it coats the back of a wooden spoon. Add sage to the
sauce and season with salt and pepper to taste. To serve,
place chicken on a plate and top with sauce.
Add freshly cut parsley as a garnish.
Italian cuisine uses the freshest ingredients to great effect
and is simple, elegant, and delicious. Italians enquire about

the food's freshness rather than its quantity. They don't understand the idea of weekly shopping; they buy their fruit and veggies every day. The amazing thing about

Italian cuisine is that there is no such thing; up until 1870, Italy was a separate federation of states.
Each region has its distinct cuisine, which has been shaped over centuries by its geography and history. For instance, due to the influence of its neighbor, the Austro-Hungarian empire, the food of the Northwest is more like that of mid-Europe. Mediterranean flavors—olive oils, fresh and dried fruit with Moorish influences, tomatoes from the New World—dominate in the South.

Read my introduction to Italian cuisine and go through the general recipes before clicking on the links to the flavors of Tuscany, Lombardy, and Sicily. Italian cuisine is the ultimate comfort food, combining a love of food with a passion for family, family life, and family events.
Italian cuisine is simple to replicate at home since it emphasizes the beauty of the ingredients rather than the chef. In general, it is flavorful and quick; even if you make your pasta, you can have a home-cooked pasta dish on the table in 30 minutes.

CHAPTER FOUR

Delicious Foie Gras, Turnip, and Potato Mille-Feuille with Wild Mushrooms

These components can be eaten on their own, with a few kinds of butter- and garlic-cooked mushrooms, or as a side dish when the pan-fried liver is being served. It is well worth the effort to make this recipe.

1 lb (450 g) (450 g) Waxy potato varieties

41/2 oz (125 g) (125 g) turnips

3 oz (75 g) (75 g) salt-free butter

7 oz (200 g) (200 g) salted and peppered foie gras, calf or chicken liver

To make the sauce:

41/2 oz (125 g) of thinly sliced mushrooms

1 tablespoon sunflower or peanut oil

Shallots, 15,

1/2 oz (15g) (15g) butter

2 fl oz (50 ml) (50 ml) sherry vinegar

2 fl oz (50 ml) (50 ml) each dry Madeira and ruby port

1/4 pt (150 ml) (150 ml) beef stock

1 stem of thyme

A little amount of dried cepes powder

1 teaspoon old sherry, salt, and pepper

Double cream or one tablespoon of truffles (optional)

As a garnish:

4 oz (110 g) of wild mushrooms, either button mushrooms or Cepes.

1/4 oz (10g) (10g) lemon juice, butter, and a sprinkling of salt

Four to five tarragon leaves and a few chervil sprigs

The potatoes should be peeled and coarsely grated before being washed, drained, and pat dried. Turnips should be peeled, grated coarsely, and added to potatoes along with three pinches of salt and pepper. 21/2 oz (65 g) of the butter should be melted, added to the mixture, and thoroughly mixed. With the remaining butter, grease the bottom of a sizable nonstick frying pan before lining it with a thin layer of turnip and potato. Using a fork, gently press down for 3–4 minutes over medium heat, turn, and crisp once more. Remove from the pan and let the excess fat drain on kitchen paper. Dry for five minutes at 275°F/140°C/gas mark 1. Stay warm.

The mushrooms must be delicately colored while being sauteed in extremely high oil to make the sauce. Three of the shallots should be finely chopped and sauteed in 1 teaspoon of butter until well-colored. The liquid will be reduced by two-thirds when the port, Madeira, and mushrooms are added, and the sherry vinegar has been heated until it has evaporated. Add the veal stock, thyme, and cepe powder, and then bring to a boil while skimming off any impurities. Sherry should be mixed with 2 fl oz (50 ml) of cold water before being strained through a fine mesh strainer to yield 4 fl oz (110 ml) of liquid. Season and taste.

The remaining 12 shallots should be peeled, chopped, and added to a roasting pan with the remaining butter, 6 tablespoons of water, and a pinch of salt. Cook for 20 minutes in the oven at 350°F/180°C/gas mark 4. As soon as the shallots are tender, reduce their juices over high heat until the shallots become a deep shade of brown and caramelize.

Clean off the mushrooms and slice them into an average size for the garnish. For one minute, sauté them in butter and salt in a pan. Check the seasoning before adding the lemon juice and tarragon.

Divide any foie gras into four pieces. Season. Cook the foie gras for 10 seconds on each side in a hot, heavy skillet. Stay warm. Seal the liver of the calf or chicken similarly, but just with a small amount of oil. Per serving, cut the liver into 4 thin slices. Divide the pancake into 12 pieces. On each of the 4 plates, start with a pancake slice in the center and top it with 2 slivers of the liver. Next, add a second pancake slice and the final 2 slivers of the liver. Add a third layer of pancakes to complete.

When the sauce is boiling, pour it over the shallots that have been caramelized. Add a tiny bit more sherry vinegar and the truffle if it needs additional acidity. Include the cream if it's too harsh. Pour over the mille-feuille, then top with chervil sprigs and mushrooms.

CHAPTER FIVE

Tempura Wild Mushrooms

This is how to prepare mushrooms perfectly every time. The best side dish for just about any main meal is these Crispy Wild Mushrooms.

READY TIME 15 minutes

25 minutes for cooking

forty minutes in total

COURSE Dinner, Side Dish

CUISINE

Mediterranean

INGREDIENTS

Wild mushrooms, 2 to 3 pounds (any kind of mushrooms works)

olive juice

kosher salt freshly cracked black pepper, and six garlic cloves, roughly chopped

1 lemon, juiced and zested

Homemade breadcrumbs in 4 teaspoons (recipe below)

1 tablespoon minced, drained, and rinsed capers

3 tablespoons chopped flat-leaf parsley

grated Parmesan or Pecorino Romano

Regarding the Breadcrumbs

4 thick slices of whole grain bread from a loaf, ripped into tiny pieces (approximately 1 12 cups when ripped)

Olive oil, two tablespoons

1/fourth cup unsalted butter

two chopped garlic cloves

1/2 kosher salt spoon

INSTRUCTIONS

Oven temperature: 425 °F.

Trim off any dry stems and wipe off any dirt from the mushrooms with a paper towel. To make the mushrooms primarily bite-sized, rip them into 1-inch slices. Put the mushrooms in a bowl and add the salt, pepper, and olive oil. Combine by tossing.

On a baking sheet with parchment paper lined, spread them out evenly. For about 20 to 25 minutes, roast, tossing once halfway through, until they are crisp around the

edges and golden brown.

Toss the mushrooms with the minced garlic, lemon zest and juice, capers, and parsley after they have been taken out of the oven. Add additional salt, pepper, heaps of shredded cheese, and handmade breadcrumbs as needed after tasting and adjusting.

Regarding the Breadcrumbs

Put the butter and olive oil in a big non-stick skillet and heat it. Incorporate the bread and cook for 3 to 5 minutes, or until the bread begins to become golden brown. Don't leave because it happens rapidly. Once aromatic, add the garlic and salt and continue to sauté for another 30 seconds or so. Remove from heat and pour any remaining oil onto a plate covered with paper towels. Use as necessary.

25

CHAPTER SIX

Sautéed Wild Mushrooms in a Hurry

Even though the recipe is straightforward, the result is incredibly nutrient-dense, rich, meaty, and earthy. In both the East and the West, wild mushrooms have long been admired for their reputedly powerful medical properties.

Ingredients: 1 pound of wild mushrooms, including Portobello, shiitake, porcini, hen of the woods, black trumpet, oyster, and lobster.

Olive oil, 3 tablespoons

2 thinly sliced shallots

2 garlic cloves, finely chopped

1/fourth cup dry white wine

2 teaspoons of chopped fresh herbs, like marjoram,

sage, thyme, and rosemary go well with mushrooms.
a half cup of chopped parsley
to taste, sea salt
black pepper, freshly ground, to taste

The Making of It
Wipe the mushrooms gently.

Remove any tough stems and discard them. (Shiitake stems are excellent for stocks but difficult to consume. Trim away any woody layer at the very bottom of mushroom clusters like hen of the woods if there is any.

Slice the mushrooms thinly—between 1/8 and 1/4 inch.

In a big skillet, warm the olive oil over medium-high heat. After cooking the shallots for a minute, add the mushrooms.

Cook the mushrooms for 8 to 10 minutes, stirring regularly until they have released their juices and started to color.

Cook for about two more minutes, until the white wine has evaporated, after stirring in the garlic.

Add the herbs, stir well, and taste-season. Add the parsley and then serve.

*Note

Numerous wild edible mushrooms have been used in cooking and have been shown to have established therapeutic benefits. Please be aware that the following information has not been reviewed by the FDA and should not be used as a replacement for professional medical advice.

Shiitake: This mushroom has been utilized for immune system modulation, liver protection, and alternative cancer and AIDS treatments.

Porcini: This mushroom is typically fortifying for systemic weakness and is regarded as a cardiovascular and metabolic tonic.

One of the monarchs of medicinal fungus is the Hen of the Woods (Maitake) mushroom. It is thought to have cancer-fighting abilities, function as a tumor inhibitor, and safeguard the liver.

Oyster: It's used to relax tendons and joints, boost the immune system, and improve veins.

Black Trumpet with Chanterelle This immune-boosting fungus is loaded with B vitamins and ostensibly suppresses the growth of tumors.

Muscles and neurons benefit from the potassium-rich portobello mushroom.

Crimini: These antioxidant-rich brown button mushrooms help cleanse the liver and prevent cancer.

Morel: This mushroom has immune-boosting, anti-inflammatory, antioxidant, and anti-tumor qualities to name a few.

CHAPTER SEVEN

Wild and Fresh Mushroom Stew

Want some wild mushrooms? I'll cook a stew primarily out of farmed mushrooms as a compromise. However, I enhance their wild flavor in a few different ways. The first step is to prepare a potent, savory broth using a few dried porcini mushrooms. The alternative is to get some authentic wild mushrooms. Even though they are expensive, a scant half-pound of chanterelles won't break the budget. Shiitake, cremini, and oyster mushrooms are used to make the last portion of the rustic stew (you can also call it a ragout). This spicy, herbaceous mushroom stew develops depth and personality as it simmers. In each bite, it conjures the familiarity of home and the primordial, whether it is spooned over spaghetti or nestled up to a soft pile of polenta.

INGREDIENTS

4 to 6 servings per batch

112 pounds of farmed brown mushrooms, such as portobello, cremini, or shiitake

12 lb. of white wild mushrooms, such as chanterelles (or use King trumpet or oyster)

virgin extra olive oil

1 big, chopped onion

Pepper and salt

1 teaspoon of thyme, chopped

1 teaspoon minced rosemary or sage

Cayenne or red pepper flakes in a pinch

1/fourth cup tomato paste

Peeled, seeded, and chopped: 3 small, ripe tomatoes

1/9 cup all-purpose flour

Use hot porcini broth or chicken or veggie broth instead.

10 grams of butter

3 minced garlic cloves

3 tablespoons finely minced parsley

Step 1 of PREPARE

Trim rough stems and clean mushrooms, keeping colors apart. Keep the stems in stock. Slice the mushrooms thinly—about 1/8 inch.

Step 2 Heat 2 tablespoons of olive oil to a warm temperature in a large skillet. Add the onion, season with salt and pepper, and stir-fry for 10 minutes, or until the onion has softened and browned. Take out of the pan and place aside.

Step 3

Turn up the heat to high and add 1 more tablespoon of oil. Add the browned mushrooms, season lightly, and stir-fry for 3 minutes or until well colored. heat setting to medium. Add tomato paste, red pepper, sage, and thyme. Cook for a minute after adding tomatoes and stirring well. Add more salt and pepper to taste. Add 1 tablespoon of the flour, whisk to combine, and cook for another minute. Add in the set-aside onions.

Step 4

Add 1 cup of mushroom broth and whisk for about a minute or until thickened. Add 1 more cup of broth gradually and simmer for 2 minutes. The sauce should have a consistency like gravy; if required, thin with more broth. the seasoning. (This part may be prepared up to several hours in advance and reheated.)

Step 5: Place butter and 1 tablespoon olive oil in a large skillet over medium-high heat just before serving. Add the chanterelles when the butter starts to turn brown, season with salt and pepper, and simmer for about 2 minutes, or until fully cooked and starting to brown. Cook for an additional minute after stirring in the garlic and parsley. Place chanterelles in a warm serving bowl after adding them to the brown mushroom mixture. If you like, serve it with pasta or polenta.

CHAPTER EIGHT

Garlic and parsley in Wild Mushrooms

The quality of your garlic and parsley is another aspect of the components to take into consideration. Never, ever, ever consider using canned, pre-chopped garlic for this (or anything for that matter in my opinion).

Pre-chopped garlic has an unpleasant flavor that, in my opinion, almost tastes fermented. It won't caramelize and softly brown like raw, freshly cut

garlic because it also contains liquid. If any of that is

in your refrigerator.

PERSILLADE TRUE (CHOP THE GARLIC AND PARSLEY TOGETHER)

Traditionally, persillade involves more than simply throwing some parsley and garlic into a pan. Garlic and parsley must be chopped together, not separately, for the most conventional outcome.

Garlic and parsley sauce, or pesto

The parsley is the same way. Only use fresh Italian flat-leaf parsley in this recipe since it genuinely has flavor. Dried parsley should only be used to garnish 1980s-era plates; otherwise, you might as well season food with sawdust.

Since flat leaf and curly parsley are about the same in price and both have little flavor, it makes sense to choose one over the other.

Hydnum umbilicated, sometimes known as hedgehog mushrooms

Here, chanterelles and hedgehogs grow well.

The kind of fat is one more point to make. There

are many different things you can try out here, and they will all have distinct outcomes for you.

Animal lards will give you a deeper flavor because they aren't flavorless, but flavorless, high heat oils like grapeseed or non-GMO canola are also acceptable options. Fat from duck and fowl is very

healthy.

Ingredients: 1 tiny clove cut fresh garlic

one tiny handful of About a half-ounce of fresh, well-dried Italian parsley

eight ounces of fresh, assorted wild mushrooms

salt of kosher to flavor

To taste, freshly ground black pepper

1 teaspoon poultry fat, especially duck fat or cooking oil

Instructions

The mushrooms should be cleaned, lightly rinsed

with water, and dried on a towel as necessary.

Use a chef's knife to finely chop the garlic and parsley on a cutting board. You will receive a small surplus from this. Persillade leftovers taste great when blended into soup or combined with hot veggies.

If you only have 10-inch saute pans, use two pans or a large cast-iron skillet to cook the water on high

while adding the mushrooms. To keep steam within, cover the pan with a lid.

Add the oil once the mushrooms have wilted and the pan is completely dry and let them softly brown.

Use salt and pepper to taste to season. Stir in a large tablespoon of the persillade after turning off the heat.

Salt should be double-checked and adjusted as necessary before the seasoning is removed and served. Just about any way you can think of, the mushrooms work well as a side dish, whether they are placed on top of a steak, a bowl of wilted greens, or a bowl of soup.

39

CHAPTER NINE

Mushrooms Roasted in Red Wine Butter

Ingredients 3 pounds of various mushrooms, including chanterelle, oyster, and cremini, cut in half if large

Canola oil, 3/4 cup plus 1 tablespoon

10 thyme leaves in a tbsp

1 teaspoon of rosemary mince

minced 1 large shallot

1 tablespoon of garlic, minced

1 cup red wine, dry

3 tablespoons cubed, cold, unsalted butter

Halal salt

Pepper

14 cups finely minced tarragon

14 cups finely minced parsley

Directions

The oven should be preheated to 400° with racks in

the upper and bottom thirds. For at least 10 minutes, preheat two big-rimmed baking sheets in the oven.

Toss the mushrooms in a sizable basin with thyme, rosemary, and 3/4 cup of oil. Spread the mushrooms evenly across the baking sheets as soon as you remove them from the oven. Roast for 25 to 30 minutes, stirring halfway during roasting, or until soft and browned.

The remaining 1 tablespoon of oil should be heated in a medium skillet in the meantime. Over moderately high heat, add the shallot and garlic and stir until softened, about 3 minutes. Add the wine and simmer for 3 to 5 minutes, or until it has reduced to a glaze. Add the butter and salt and pepper to taste.

Place each mushroom on its baking sheet. Stir well

after adding the red wine butter. Add salt and pepper and mix once more. Serve in a bowl with the tarragon and parsley sprinkled on top.

Plan ahead

Both the red wine butter and the roasted mushrooms can be stored in the refrigerator overnight. Before mixing and adding the herbs immediately before serving, slightly reheat the mushrooms.

CHAPTER TEN

Salad of Warm Mushrooms with Bacon Vinegar

Ingredients

Extra virgin olive oil, half a cup

50 ml of vegetable oil

1 head of garlic, crushed but unpeeled cloves

1 pound of assorted wild mushrooms, including oyster, enoki, and shiitake, with thickly sliced caps in place of the thick stems.

Freshly ground pepper and salt

Pecans, 3/4 cup

bacon is sliced thickly and divided crosswise into 1/4-inch pieces.

1 leek, finely cut, white and tender green portions

50 ml of cider vinegar

1 teaspoon molasses or sorghum

1 teaspoon of lemon juice, fresh

6 ounces of robust baby greens, such as spinach, arugula, mustard, or tatsoi

3 ounces of crumbled cold, fresh goat cheese

Directions

Set the oven to 425 degrees. Bring the garlic and both oils to a simmer in a pot. Cook for 15 minutes at low heat until aromatic. Remove the garlic from the oil and discard it.

Add 6 tablespoons of the garlic oil to a large bowl with the mushrooms and season with salt and pepper. (Save the leftover garlic oil for another time.) When the mushrooms are crisp and golden, roast them for 35 minutes, stirring once or twice. On a pie plate, spread the pecans out and toast for 7 minutes, or until aromatic. Cool down.

Cook the bacon until crisp in a big skillet over medium heat, turning often, for about 8 minutes. Transfer the bacon to a dish covered in paper towels using a slotted spoon. Return half of the fat to the skillet after straining it into a heatproof bowl. Over medium-low heat, add the leek to the skillet and simmer for about 6 minutes, or until tender. Add the vinegar and boil for 5 minutes, or until it has been reduced to 3 tablespoons. Whisk in the leftover bacon grease, sorghum, and lemon juice after turning the heat off.

Mix the greens, vinaigrette, mushrooms, and pecans in a big bowl. Add salt and pepper and mix once more. After serving, top with goat cheese and bacon.

CHAPTER ELEVEN

Goat cheese with Dried Porcini Mushroom Risotto

Ingredients

1 cup dried mushrooms, such as dry porcini mushrooms (about 1 ounce)

3 cups of hot water, plus more if necessary

3 1/2 cups of homemade stock or low-sodium

commercial chicken broth, plus more as necessary.

Olive oil, 3 tablespoons

one sliced onion

5 minced garlic cloves

Arborio rice, two cups

Salt, 1 1/4 teaspoons

Butter, two tablespoons

freshly ground black pepper, 1/4 teaspoon

2 ounces of crumbled mild goat cheese, such as

Montrachet

for serving, parmesan cheese

Directions

Pour the hot water over the dried mushrooms in a medium bowl. For around 20 minutes, soak to soften. Chop the mushrooms after removing them from the liquid they had been soaking in. Pour the liquid into a medium saucepan after straining it through a paper towel-lined sieve. Simmer the broth in the pan after adding it.

Heat the oil over moderately low heat in a medium pot. Cook the onion and garlic for about 5 minutes, stirring periodically, until the onion is transparent. Stir the rice, salt, and chopped mushrooms for about two minutes, or until the rice starts to turn opaque.

About 1/2 cup of the simmering stock should be added to the rice, and it should be cooked while regularly stirring until the broth is completely absorbed. Rice and broth should softly bubble; change the heat as necessary. As you continue to cook the rice, add the broth 1/2 cup at a time, letting

the rice absorbs each cup before adding the next. This method should take the rice between 25 and 30 minutes to cook thoroughly. The starch from the rice should thicken any remaining broth that hasn't been absorbed. You might not need to use the entire amount of liquid, or you could require additional broth or water.

Add the goat cheese, butter, and pepper after mixing. Add grated Parmesan to the risotto before serving.

CHAPTER TWELVE

Baked eggs with spinach and mushrooms

Ingredients

Olive oil, 1 tbsp

1 large leek, chopped into 1/2-inch pieces, with just the white and light green parts.

1/fourth cup unsalted butter

1 pound of finely sliced white or cremini mushrooms (about 6 cups)

a serving of soy sauce

14 cups of dry red wine

Baby spinach, 5 ounces

Freshly ground pepper and salt

Four big eggs

Four slices of whole-grain bread

Directions

Set the oven to 350 degrees. Olive oil should be

heated in a large skillet. Leeks should be added and cooked for three minutes while stirring at moderate heat. Add the mushrooms and butter and stir. For 7 minutes, with the lid on, simmer the mushrooms until they soften, and a lot of liquid is released. Remove the cover, add the soy sauce, and then cook for 5 minutes, stirring occasionally, until the liquid has reduced to 2 tablespoons. Add the spinach and stir for 2 minutes, or until wilted. Add salt and pepper to taste.

Four 1-cup ramekins or little gratin plates should be oil-coated. Place one egg on top of each ramekin after adding the mushrooms and spinach. When the white is barely set and the yolks are runny, bake for 10 to 12 minutes. Serve beside the bread after 2 minutes of standing.

Notes

One serving contains 323 calories, 13 grams of fat, 4.2 grams of saturated fat, 35 grams of carbohydrates, 6 grams of fiber, and 16 grams of protein.

55

CHAPTER THIRTEEN

Crostini with mushrooms and Fontina

Ingredients \Four diagonally divided slices of peasant bread that are half an inch thick.

Extra virgin olive oil, 5 teaspoons

1.5 lbs of white mushrooms

Unsalted butter, two teaspoons

2 medium shallots, chopped finely

1 big clove of minced garlic

1 teaspoon of thyme, chopped

water, 3 tablespoons

Freshly ground pepper and salt

1/4 pound of coarsely shredded Fontina cheese (about 1 cup)

a tbsp. of minced parsley

Directions

Preheat the oven to 400°. Arrange the bread on a

baking sheet and drizzle with 3 tablespoons of olive oil. Toast for 12 minutes, until slightly golden around the edges. Turn the broiler on.

Slice the mushrooms very thinly in the interim. The butter should be cooked for two minutes over high heat in a big skillet to lightly brown it. Mushrooms and the remaining 2 tablespoons of olive oil should be added, and they should be cooked for 2 minutes without being stirred. For the next 10 minutes, simmer the mixture, stirring regularly, until it is evenly browned. Add the shallots, garlic, and thyme, reduce the heat to medium and simmer for 5 minutes, or until the shallots are soft. Cook for an additional three minutes after adding the water and scraping off any browned bits from the pan's bottom. After giving the mushrooms a salt and pepper seasoning, turn off the heat.

Place the cheese on top of the toast after adding the mushroom mixture. For two minutes, or until the cheese is melted, broil the dish. Place the crostini on a platter, top with parsley, and then serve

59

CHAPTER FOURTEEN

Pizza with Portobello mushrooms and red peppers

Ingredients

Olive oil, 6 teaspoons

1 red bell pepper, thinly sliced; 2

1 1/2 pounds of stemmed, quarter-inch-thick-sliced

portobello mushrooms.

1 salt shaker

1 pound of either homemade or bought pizza dough

3 minced garlic cloves

freshly ground black pepper, 1/4 teaspoon

chopped, 3/4 cup of basil leaves, lightly packed

1/4-inch cubes of fresh, salty mozzarella, weighing half a pound

grated Parmesan, half a cup

Directions

the oven to 450 degrees. 3 tablespoons of the oil

should be heated over moderately high heat in a sizable frying pan. Peppers should be added to the pan and cooked for 10 minutes while occasionally stirring. For an additional 10 minutes, add the salt and mushrooms and continue to simmer while stirring regularly until the mushrooms are browned.

Oil a large baking sheet or a 14-inch pizza pan in the meantime. Shape the pizza dough into a 9-by-13-inch rectangle or a 14-inch round and press it onto the pan.

The pizza dough should be covered in peppers and mushrooms. For 12 minutes, bake. Basil, black pepper, and garlic should be sprinkled on. Add the mozzarella first, followed by the Parmesan. Add the final 3 tablespoons of oil in a drizzle. For a further 10 to 15 minutes, bake until the cheese is bubbling and starting to brown.

63

CHAPTER FIFTEEN

Wild Mushroom Sourdough Dressing, Vegetarian

1 1/2 pounds of rustic sourdough bread, broken into 1-inch pieces, as the main ingredient

Unsalted butter, divided into 1/2 cup and 2 teaspoons (5 ounces), with enough for dish greasing

2 cups of celery, chopped

two cups of yellow onion, diced

1 teaspoon of fresh thyme chopped finely.

1 tablespoon of fresh rosemary chopped finely.

2 pounds of freshly cut, quarter-inch-thick slices of a variety of fresh wild mushrooms, including chanterelle, oyster, trumpet, and hen-of-the-woods. Tough stems should be cut off and discarded.

1 tablespoon sherry, dry

14 cups chopped; fresh flat-leaf parsley packed in a cup

A teaspoon or two of kosher salt

1 teaspoon of black pepper, ground

3 cups of vegetable stock, either handmade or purchased (such as Brodo Seaweed Mushroom Broth)

two huge eggs.

Directions
Spread the bread slices out in a single layer on three-rimmed baking pans and let them unattended to dry out for eight hours or overnight.

Turn on the 375°F oven. In a deep 13 to 14-inch skillet over medium heat, melt 2 tablespoons of butter until it begins to sizzle. Add the celery and onion; simmer, stirring

frequently, for 10 to 13 minutes, or until slightly softened. Thyme and rosemary should be added. Cook for one minute, stirring constantly, until fragrant. Then pour the celery mixture into a big bowl.

Clean the skillet, then add 1/4 cup butter. Heat till sizzling on medium. Add mushrooms and stir. Turn the heat up to high and sauté the mushrooms for about 3 minutes, stirring occasionally, until the bottoms are browned. Mushrooms should be stirred often during the 20 minutes it takes for them to completely brown. Turn off the stovetop and let the skillet stand for 30 seconds. Sherry should be added to the skillet while swirling and scraping any browned bits off the bottom. Reset the skillet to medium heat and stir in the remaining 1/4 cup butter, parsley, salt, and pepper. A mixture of celery and mushrooms should be combined, then dried bread should be added.

Stock and eggs should be properly combined in a whisk. Slowly add the stock mixture to the bread mixture while stirring continuously. Stir continuously until most of the stock is absorbed. Spoon the bread mixture into a baking dish that has been greased with butter and covered with aluminum foil securely.

For about 30 minutes, bake in a preheated oven until

thoroughly heated. After 15 to 20 minutes of cooking, remove the cover. 10 minutes should pass before serving.

67

CHAPTER SIXTEEN

Braised Pork Loin with Wine and Mushrooms

Ingredients

1 (2-pound) boneless center-cut pork loin, tied with kitchen twine

1 1/2 teaspoons coarse sea salt

1/2 teaspoon black pepper

3 tablespoons olive oil

1 pound white button mushrooms, quartered

8 small white spring onions (about 10 ounces), trimmed,

white parts only

3 large garlic cloves, smashed

1/2 cup (4 ounces) Corsican Muscat wine

1 cup lower-sodium chicken stock

3 rosemary sprigs

6 thyme sprigs

8 (3-inch) orange peel strips

Cooked polenta, for serving
Directions
Set the oven to 400 °F. Salt and pepper meat in a uniform layer. Large ovenproof skillet or Dutch oven with medium-high heat for oil.

Add the pork to the pan and cook, stirring occasionally, for 3 minutes or until golden brown on one side. Spit pork. Repeat these steps for 12 minutes or until each side is browned. Take the pork out of the pan and set it aside. Add the mushrooms, onions, and garlic to the pan; cook over medium-high, stirring frequently, for about 8 minutes, or until the liquid from the mushrooms has

released and evaporated. Add the wine and simmer for about 5 minutes, scraping up any browned bits from the bottom of the pan. Add the stock, thyme, and rosemary and simmer for 3 minutes without stirring. Pork should be added back to the pan. Cover, place in the preheated oven, and roast for about 30 minutes, or until a thermometer placed in the center of the thickest part of the meat reads 130°F.

pan from the oven. Move the pork to a chopping board and give it five minutes to rest. Add orange peel strips to the mushroom mixture in the pan in the meantime. Over medium-high heat, bring to a boil. Boil for about 3 minutes, or until the sauce has slightly thickened. Throw away the thyme, rosemary, and orange peel strips.

Remove and discard the pork's string. Slice the pork diagonally. Serve the mushroom mixture over polenta.

CHAPTER SEVENTEEN

Chicken and mushrooms in a sheet pan with a parsley sauce

ingredients.
1 1/2 pounds of skinless, boneless chicken thighs

Halal salt

Pepper

2 tablespoons and half a cup of extra-virgin olive oil

1 pound of various mushrooms, including cremini and

shiitake stemmed and, if large, cut in half.

1 thinly sliced lemon, with extra slices for decoration

1/2 cup of parsley, plus additional for garnish

Red wine vinegar, 2 teaspoons

1 big clove of minced garlic
Directions
A big-rimmed baking sheet should be heated in the oven at 450 degrees. Sprinkle plenty of salt and pepper on both sides of the chicken. 2 tablespoons of olive oil should be drizzled onto the hot baking sheet. Place the chicken on the heated sheet in a single layer and roast for 5 minutes or until the chicken starts to brown.

2 tablespoons of olive oil should be mixed with the mushrooms and lemon slices in a medium bowl before being equally distributed around the chicken in the oven. Roast for about 30 minutes, or until the chicken is cooked through and the mushrooms and lemon are browned.
In the meantime, combine the remaining 6 tablespoons of olive oil, 1/2 cup of parsley, vinegar, and garlic in a small bowl. Add salt to the sauce.

Place the lemon slices, mushrooms, and chicken in a dish. Add a little of the sauce and top with lemon and parsley

for decoration. Pass the remaining sauce around the table as you serve.

Serve alongside a green salad and quinoa.

75

CONCLUSION

Where can I discover wild edible mushrooms? is the fundamental and most important question that each person who is urged to go mushroom hunting asks himself. If you want to be a successful wild mushroom hunter, you must be aware of the finest locations to look for wild edible mushrooms.

We all know that there are numerous mushrooms in wooded areas (I won't discuss those in fields for the time being). However, there is a thing to consider: not every tree in a forest develops a mycosis with fungus (mushrooms), particularly edible ones. As a result, mushrooms grow in symbiosis with specific trees, which is undoubtedly one of the reasons why it can be difficult to find wild edible mushrooms. Therefore, the types of wild mushrooms that will grow in a forest are determined by the trees and climate.

It is advised to conduct some planning before going mushroom hunting. Investigation of the forest type (exactly what trees grow there) within a reachable range should be the first item on the planning list. According to my personal prior experiences, fir, oak, and birch trees make the best combination of trees since they are the only ones that can create the ideal conditions for the most delicious Boletus fungi to develop.

I take note of the different kinds and numbers of trees in the area each time I harvest a mushroom. Although there might be areas with a greater concentration of one of those species, it is extremely nice when the forest is made up of a proportionate blend of fir trees, oaks, and birches.

The land that fungal spores can accommodate themselves in is made by plants. The soil may be coated in the trees' needles if you are near spruce and pine trees. You would mostly be under the shade of these tall trees, whose lower branches would be barren of needles or missing altogether. The terrain would appear to be dry. This kind of dirt might make you feel as though you've trodden on a sponge because it is pliable and squishy. The area will be covered in green moss if there is enough room between the trees for direct sunlight to enter. It is preferable to go out there directly after a sequence of rainy days followed by sunny ones if you want to find wild edible mushrooms among the spruce and pine trees.

The bottom is mostly covered by fall leaves, broken

branches, dead stuff, and grass if you're near oak or birch trees. Along the edge of a birch forest, taller grass frequently causes you to trip. Sunlight spots will occasionally appear as the sun's rays pass through the tree trunks. You can frequently find bushes of wild raspberries nearby. You are enticed to look around those trees and amid the grass by the unforgettable scent of fresh ground and fungus, which gives you hope that some edible mushrooms may be close. Just be sure to search cautiously.

As a general conclusion, I'd want to state that there isn't any one region or location that has the greatest abundance of wild edible mushrooms. Instead, they spread out and change from year to year. They may arrive out of nowhere in a location where they had not been spotted recently or for a very long period. In general, finding wild edible mushrooms depends entirely on your luck and your knowledge of the forest. And for that reason, I enjoy searching for and discovering wild edible mushrooms.